SUPER SHARKS

A LEGO® ADVENTURE IN THE REAL WORLD

Let's dive in and spot some sharks!

■ SCHOLASTIC

New York Toronto London Auckland
Sydney Mexico City New Delhi Hong Kong

Welcome, LEGO fans!

LEGO® minifigures show you the world in a unique nonfiction program.

This leveled reader is part of a program of LEGO® nonfiction books, with something for all the family, at every age and stage. LEGO nonfiction books have amazing facts, beautiful real-world photos, and minifigures everywhere, leading the fun and discovery.

To find out more about the books in the program, visit www.scholastic.com.

Leveled readers from Scholastic are designed to support your child's efforts to learn how to read at every age and stage.

LEVEL 1 READER

Beginning reader
Preschool–Grade 1
Sight words
Words to sound out
Simple sentences

LEVEL 2 READER

Developing reader
Grades 1–2
New vocabulary
Longer sentences

LEVEL 3 READER

Growing reader
Grades 1–3
Reading for inspiration and information

Come find out all about sharks.

Sharks are super fish! Their streamlined bodies make them super fast, and they are super hunters.

Sharks have been on Earth for 420 million years. They came before dinosaurs!

Sharks rarely hurt people. They're awesome!

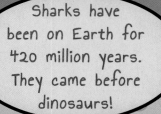

Let's go meet some sharks!

BUILD IT!
Build a boat to go shark spotting.

The smallest sharks are about as long as an adult's hand. The biggest are as long as a bus!

There are 500 different types of sharks.

A shortfin mako shark moves its tail from side to side to push through the water. It's the fastest shark in the world.

Splash! It swims at 60 miles per hour (96 km/h).

BUILD IT!
Build an underwater lab. Now your scientist minifigures can study speedy makos.

Makos can also leap right out of the water. Gulp . . .

The hammerhead shark's eyes are on the side of its head. As it swims, it moves its head from side to side to see all around.

I think hammerheads look awesome!

Shark coming!
Where shall I
hide?

You can't hide.
Sharks sense
electricity in
your body.

I have electricity?
Cool! I guess I'm
super, too!

Hammerheads
can sense tasty fish
from a mile away.

The hammerhead
shark is on the hunt.
It's hungry for
smaller fish, squid,
or shellfish.

The great white shark is one of the biggest sharks in the ocean. It can grow to 20 feet (6 m) long.

Great whites eat seals, sea lions, and even small whales.

Great whites swim all the time, even when they're sleeping!

The hungry great white shark opens its huge mouth. It has 300 sharp teeth, each 3 inches (7.5 cm) long.

Sharks' teeth often fall out, so they grow new ones.

Sharks can have 30,000 teeth in a lifetime!

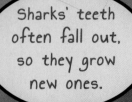

Great whites don't chew food. They bite off chunks or swallow it whole.

BUILD IT!
Great whites are fast! Build a boat or submarine that is even faster. How fast can it go?

Great whites don't need to eat every day.

Yum! Hungry copper sharks spot a shoal of fish. The fish swim in a ball to protect themselves. But, the sharks just swim through the ball and grab mouthfuls of fish!

Some sharks also eat penguins!

Most sharks prefer to work alone.

But they may work together to catch big prey.

Let's get that banana!

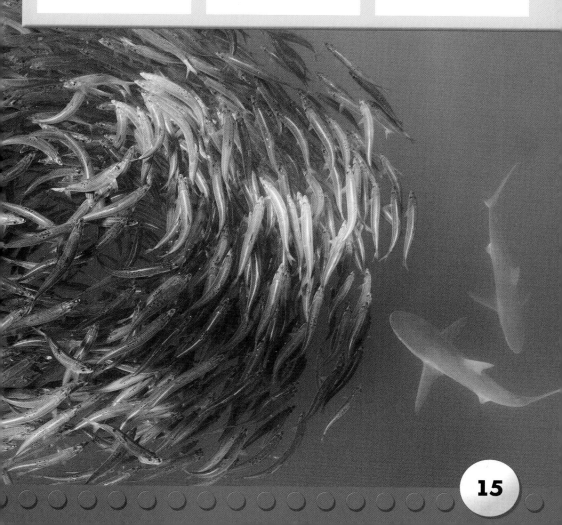

Baby tiger sharks have stripes, but they fade as they get older.

The tiger shark is looking for food. Its favorite snacks are fish, jellyfish, turtles, sea birds, and even other sharks. Tiger sharks eat almost anything, including garbage!

BUILD IT!

Build an underwater viewing station to watch tiger sharks from. Make sure they don't eat it!

Tiger sharks are sometimes called garbage cans with fins!

Well at least they clean the place up!

CALIFORNIA 47
73 69

Meet the biggest fish in the world. The whale shark can be as long as a school bus. But it only eats tiny sea creatures, such as krill and plankton.

A whale shark has 300 rows of tiny teeth. But it doesn't even chew food!

A hungry whale shark swims with its mouth open.

It sucks or gulps food in. Cool!

Yuck! I will bring you a spoon!

Some sharks make long trips called migrations. They migrate to find food, or a safe place to have pups.

Scientists put electronic tags on sharks to track their migrations.

Hammerhead sharks can travel up to 1,800 miles (3,000 km).

BUILD IT!
Plan a minifigure migration! Build a boat or plane. Where will they go, and how will they get there?

One great white, named "Lydia", has traveled more than 36,000 miles (58,000 km).

Shark babies are called pups. Some shark pups grow inside their moms. Other types of sharks lay eggs in special cases.

Lemon sharks have up to 17 pups at one time.

The egg cases
look like
little bags!

A shark's egg case is called a mermaid's purse.

Strange sharks live on the ocean floor. Check out the sawshark's long snout!

The sawshark slashes its prey with its chainsaw snout. S-awesome!

sawshark

Wobbegongs hide in the rocks and sand. They pounce on prey as it swims past!

BUILD IT!
Build a super-strong submarine that can dive to the ocean floor. Go spot some strange sharks!

wobbegong

Yikes! I hope wobbegongs don't like hot dogs . . .

25

Deep in the ocean there is no light. Cookiecutter sharks have lights on their bellies to attract prey.

cookiecutter shark

The cookiecutter shark makes cookiecutter-shaped bites on its prey.

The goblin shark pushes its jaws out to grab its prey. Crunch!

It's so dark down here. I can't see any sharks!

The lanternshark's body lights up. Look!

A glow-in-the-dark shark! Awesome!

The goblin shark has a super long snout that helps to sense prey.

goblin shark

Coral reefs are home to about two million different types of sea creatures. Sharks feed on most of them!

Hey, sharks! Let's be friends.

Actually, sharks can attack other sharks.

Yikes! I'm off to change my suit!

Sharks hunt shrimp, squid, lobsters, and crabs on the reef.

BUILD IT!
Build a super shark. How big is it? How many teeth does it have? What does it eat?

Build a LEGO® underwater world

Use your stickers to create a shark-tastic ocean adventure!

Super shark words

coral reef
A rock-like ridge in the ocean formed by the growth and deposit of coral skeletons and other substances.

electronic tag
A small object attached to a shark that sends out an electronic signal so scientists can see where the shark goes.

krill
Tiny shrimp-like creatures that are an important food for some sharks, especially whale sharks.

migration
To move from one place to another at different times of the year. Animals usually migrate to find food or have babies.

plankton
Tiny living things that live in the ocean and are carried along by ocean currents.

prey
An animal that is hunted by another animal for food.

pup
A baby shark.

shoal
A group of fish.

snout
A long nose that sticks out.

streamlined
A smooth shape that makes movement through water easier.

Sharks are super awesome, but they can't surf!

Index

A, B
ball of fish   14, 15

C
cookiecutter shark   26
coral reef   28, 29
crab   29

D, E
dinosaurs   4
eggs   23
eyes   8, 9

F, G
garbage can   16
goblin shark   27
great white shark   10, 11, 12, 13

H, I, J
hammerhead shark   8, 9
jellyfish   16

K, L
krill   18
lantern shark   27
lemon shark   22, 23
lobster   29

M, N
mako shark   6, 7
mermaid's purse   23
migration   20, 21

O, P, Q
penguins   14
plankton   18
pups   22

R, S
sawshark   24
sea lions   11
shrimp   29
sizes of sharks   5
squid   29

T, U, V
teeth   12, 18, 22
tiger shark   16, 17
turtles   16

W, X, Y Z
whale shark   18, 19
whales   11
wobbegong   25

Credits

The publishers would like to thank the following. For the LEGO Group: Randi Kirsten Sørensen, Senior Editorial Coordinator; Paul Hansford, Creative Publishing Manager; Martin Leighton Lindhardt, Publishing Graphic Designer; and Heidi K. Jensen Business Manager. For their help in making this book: Kim Bryan, Neal Cobourne, John Goldsmid, Jana Herko, Sharri Joffe, Rachel Phillipson, Ali Scrivens, and Bryn Walls.

Photos ©: cover top left: frantisek hojdysz/Fotolia; cover center: Wildestanimal/Alamy Images; cover center right: Hoatzinexp/iStockphoto; cover-back cover background: yigitdenizozdemir/iStockphoto; cover bottom right: strmko/iStockphoto; 1: Rodrigo Friscione/Getty Images; 3: Alexander Safonov/Getty Images; 4-5 background and throughout: cosmin4000/iStockphoto; 4-5 shark: by wildestanimal/Getty Images; 6-7: Richard Robinson/Getty Images; 7 inset: by wildestanimal/Getty Images; 8-9 background: Martin Strmiska/Alamy Images; 8 left: EXTREME-PHOTOGRAPHER/iStockphoto; 8 right: frantisek hojdysz/Fotolia; 10: Andrea Izzotti/Shutterstock; 11: Wildestanimal/Alamy Images; 12-13 background: Rost-9D/iStockphoto; 12 shark: Carlos Villoch - MagicSea.com/Alamy Images; 13 shark: Carlos Villoch - MagicSea.com/Alamy Images; 14-15: Pete Oxford/Minden Pictures/Getty Images; 16-17 top: NaluPhoto/iStockphoto; 16 boots: Ericlefrancais/iStockphoto; 16 tire: jack-sooksan/iStockphoto; 16 license plate: stone18/iStockphoto; 18-19: Migration Media - Underwater Imaging/Getty Images; 20-21 bottom: Hoatzinexp/iStockphoto; 20-21 top: Alexander Safonov/Getty Images; 21 top: lindsay_imagery/iStockphoto; 22-23 background: richcarey/iStockphoto; 22 center: Michael Patrick O'Neill/www.mpostock.com; 22-23 kelp: Shur_ca/iStockphoto; 23 top: D.P. Wilson/FLPA/Science Source; 24 right: WaterFrame/Alamy Images; 24-25 background: valio84sl/iStockphoto; 24 left: Stephen Frink Collection/Alamy Images; 26 top: Bill Curtsinger/Getty Images; 26-27 bottom: Kelvin Aitken/VWPics/Alamy Images; 28 coral reef: Damocean/iStockphoto; 28 hermit crab: GlobalP/iStockphoto; 28 sharks: richcarey/iStockphoto; 28-29 background: ultramarinfoto/iStockphoto; 28 red coral: scubaluna/iStockphoto; 29 squid: inusuke/iStockphoto; 29 fish: Damocean/iStockphoto; 29 shark: ShaneGross/iStockphoto; 29 turtle: cinoby/iStockphoto; 30 bottom: lindsay_imagery/iStockphoto; 31 top: adventtr/iStockphoto.

All LEGO illustrations and stickers by Paul Lee.

> Sharks are super, but I'm king of the ocean!

Written by Penny Arlon, designed by Victoria Gordon-Harris, and illustrated by Paul Lee.

978-1-338-26193-6

10 9 8 7 6 5 4   18 19 20 21 22

Made in USA

First edition, July 2018

> How do you make a shark laugh? Tell a whale of a tale.

> A shark grows over 20,000 teeth in its lifetime. That's worth a smile!

Dive into the world of sharks with the LEGO® minifigures.

Check out these awesome animals, and discover their amazing underwater world.

You'll find great LEGO building ideas, too!

PRE 1 READER
ABC's & first words.

LEVEL 1 READER
Sight words, words to sound out & simple sentences.

LEVEL 2 READER
New vocabulary & longer sentences.

LEVEL 3 READER
Reading for inspiration & information.

Based on the best research about how children learn to read, Scholastic Readers are developed under the supervision of reading experts and are educator approved.

■SCHOLASTIC
www.scholastic.com

APPEALS TO **K-2nd GRADERS**

READING LEVEL **GRADE 1**

More leveling information for this book: www.scholastic.com/readinglevel

CE

Scholastic Inc., 557 Broadway, New York, NY 100
Scholastic UK Ltd., Euston House, Eversholt Street, London NW1 1
Made in USA / Fabriqué en Etats-U

5+ $4.99 US / $6.99 C

ISBN 978-1-338-26193-6
50499
9 781338 261936